Let's Go Explore

EGYPT

Written by Kim Washburn

ZONDERkidz

ZONDERKIDZ

Egypt
Copyright © 2014 by Zondervan

This title is also available as a Zondervan ebook.

Requests for information should be addressed to:

Zonderkidz, 3900 *Sparks Drive SE, Grand Rapids, MI 49546*

Library of Congress Cataloging-in-Publication Data

Washburn, Kim, 1970-
    Let's go explore Egypt / written by Kim Washburn.
        pages cm
    ISBN 978-0-310-74315-6 (softcover)
    1. Egypt—Juvenile literature. 2. Egypt—Civilization—To 332 B.C.—Juvenile literature.
  I. Title. II. Title: Let us go explore Egypt.
DT49.W35 2014 2014
962—dc23   2013030051

Written by: Kim Washburn
Editor: Mary Hassinger
Art direction: Deborah Washburn
Cover and interior design: Jody Langley
Title page photography: © 1995 by Phoenix Data Systems

Printed in China

18 19 20 21 22 23 /LPC/ 22 21 20 19 18 17 16 15 14 13 12 11 10 9 8 7 6 5 4 3 2

WELCOME TO
EGYPT

The world's first great civilization

TABLE OF CONTENTS

MAP OF EGYPT

Egypt spans two continents.

ASIA

AFRICA

LIBYA

E C

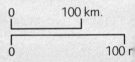

0   100 km.

0   100 r

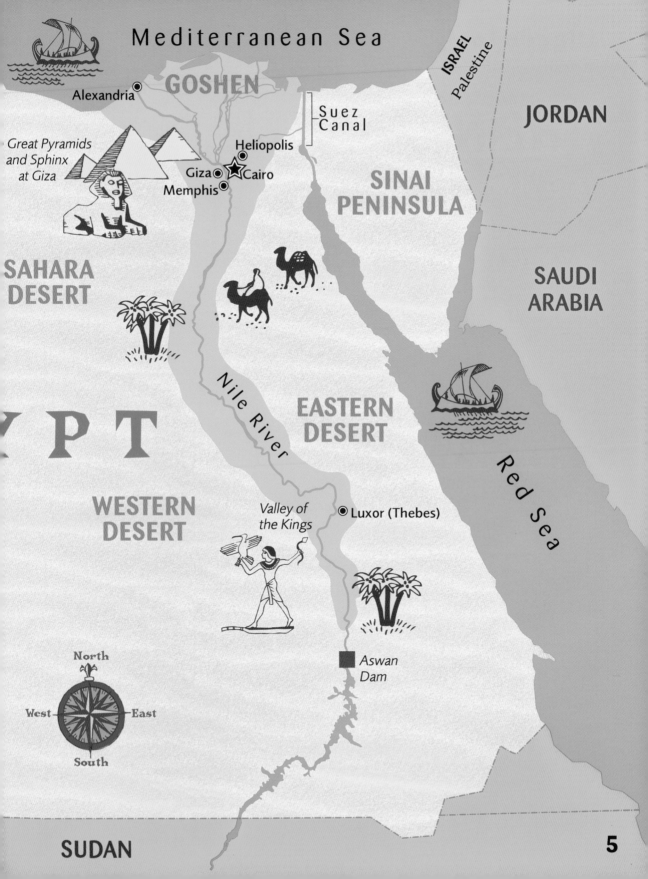

Mediterranean Sea

GOSHEN

Alexandria

ISRAEL
Palestine

JORDAN

Suez
Canal

Great Pyramids
and Sphinx
at Giza

Heliopolis

Giza ☆ Cairo
Memphis

SINAI
PENINSULA

SAHARA
DESERT

SAUDI
ARABIA

EASTERN
DESERT

Nile River

YPT

Red Sea

WESTERN
DESERT

Valley of
the Kings

Luxor (Thebes)

North

Aswan
Dam

West   East

South

SUDAN

THE NILE FILE

Miles of Nile

The only river in Egypt is also the longest river in the world. Almost all Egyptians live along the great, green Nile that winds through the country.

The Vital Nile

The Nile naturally floods every year, giving the land fresh, fruitful soil. The grain grown in the region then gets the entire winter to mature without needing more water. This is good for thirsty land that sees little rain the rest of the year.

The Nile River: photo from space

© Oleg Zhukov/www.istockphoto.com

Set Sail

Egypt's hot, dry landscape is great for scorpions but not for people taking supplies a long distance. But hop in a boat to ride the Nile, and the journey is faster and easier.

NASA

DEA/G. DAGLI ORTI/Getty Images

Go with the Flow

Most major rivers run toward the equator, the line that cuts the Earth in half. Not the Nile! It flows north toward the Mediterranean Sea. Hieroglyphics show what ancient sailors knew: the picture for traveling downstream shows a boat riding the current with an oar and a folded sail. The hieroglyph for traveling upstream with the south wind shows a boat with a full sail.

Wonder on the Water

A few thousand years ago, an Egyptian princess pulled a manmade papyrus basket from the Nile. Inside was a baby boy. "She named him Moses, saying 'I drew him out of the water'" (Exodus 2:10). God's miraculous plans continued years later when Moses left Egypt through another body of water, the Red Sea.

DEA/A. DAGLI ORTI/Getty Images

Hieroglyph
The Nile River

7

THE SUEZ AND THE SEA

Little Canal, Big Job

The Suez Canal separates two continents, joins two seas, and maintains a connection between the East and the West. Much of the world's sea trade goes through the canal.

Suez Canal

Water Works

The sea is an easy route to transport whopping loads of important things, including oil for heating and grain for eating. Throughout the ages, different nations took over the Mediterranean Sea to control the sea trade. Under Roman rule for example, Egypt supplied corn that the entire Roman Empire needed, by way of the sea.

DEA Picture Library/Getty Images

Hieroglyph
Sail

Short and Sweet

It took ten years to build the **Suez Canal**, a waterway that connects the Mediterranean Sea with the Red Sea. Now boats can travel between Europe and Asia without going all the way around Africa. The shortcut saves time and money!

Sea It

The **Mediterranean Sea** touches the Atlantic Ocean, but mostly it is surrounded by land, which explains its name. *Mediterraneus* is Latin for "middle of the earth."

IN THE ZONE

Upper and Lower Egypt

For ages Egypt was considered "Two Lands." The water lily (or lotus) symbolized the Upper region and the native papyrus plant symbolized the Lower.

Israelites of the Bible settled in Lower Egypt, in the eastern delta area of Goshen. Pharaohs of the Bible generally settled in the temples of Upper Egypt.

Four Regions

1 **Nile Valley and Delta**—Historically, most cities and palaces were built on the east side of the Nile River, the side where the sun rises. Tombs were built on the west side where the sun sets.

2 **Western Desert**—Locals often referred to the sandy deserts as the "Red Land" and the fruitful Nile Valley as the "Black Land."

3 **Eastern Desert**—Summer months in the desert can bring 120-degree Fahrenheit days.

4 **Sinai Peninsula**—Most of Egypt is on the continent of Africa, but this knob of land is on the continent of Asia. The southern tip of the Sinai Peninsula is the traditional site of Mount Sinai. Some experts think God gave the Ten Commandments to Moses on this mountain, some believe on a mountain farther north, and still others think it is even farther east.

© photo-oasis/Shutt

North Wind Picture Archives/Alamy

North Wind Picture Archives/A

0   100 km.

0   100 m

DEA Picture Library/
Getty Images

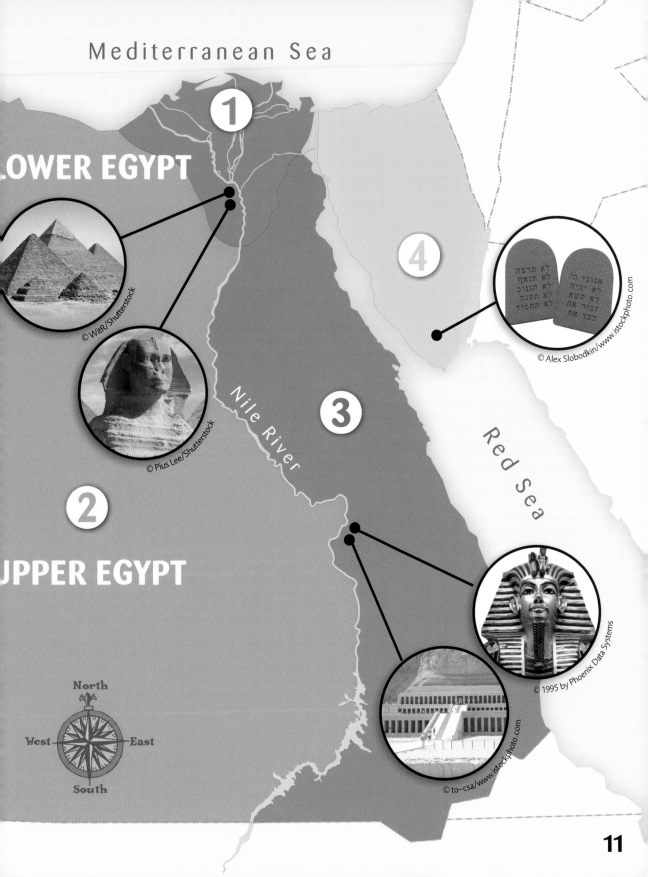

Mediterranean Sea

LOWER EGYPT

© WitR/Shutterstock

© Pius Lee/Shutterstock

2

UPPER EGYPT

North

West — East

South

Nile River

3

Red Sea

© to–csa/www.istockphoto.com

4

לא תרצח לא
תנאף לא תגנוב
לא תענה לא
תחמד

אנכי ה' לא
יהיה לא תשא
זכור את כבד את

© Alex Slobodkin/www.istockphoto.com

© 1995 by Phoenix Data Systems

WITH A CAPITAL C

Center of Attention

Cairo, the capital of Egypt, is one of the largest cities on the continent of Africa. There are more than nine million people living in an area that's twice the size of Washington DC, the capital of the United States.

Amazing Antiques

Royal mummies, stone statues, delicate papyrus, and the solid gold mask of King Tutankhamun rest in Cairo's **Museum of Egyptian Antiquities** along with more than 100,000 other priceless artifacts.

Baker Photo Archive. The Egyptian Ministry of Antiquities. The Cairo Museum

A **bazaar** is a Middle Eastern market with rows of shops or stalls called *souks*.

What Money *Khan* Buy

In a 600-year-old structure, Cairo hosts **Khân al-Khalîli**. Enjoying street food and coffee shops, locals and tourists wander the aisles of this historic bazaar, listen to artisans bang on decorated copper trays, or pop into shops that sell rugs and jugs and everything in between.

Old Meets New

A modern city with medieval history, travelers to Cairo can see ancient relics and more than 400 historic monuments, including mosques, tombs, and massive stone gates that allowed entry into the city in medieval times.

CELEBRATED CITIES

Pearl of the Mediterranean

Alexandria served as Egypt's capital city for 300 years. Now it serves as Egypt's main seaport. The Lighthouse of Alexandria was named one of the Seven Wonders of the Ancient World before it was destroyed by an earthquake in 1323.

Archives Charmet/The Bridgeman Art Library

World's Greatest Open-Air Museum

Ancient Thebes is now called **Luxor**. As many as 30 pharaohs are a part of the Karnak Temple Complex, the largest ancient religious site in the world.

Wikimedia commons

14

City of the Sun

One of the oldest cities in Egypt, ancient Heliopolis, was the capital of the province of Goshen. Grain was stored here during the seven-year famine during Joseph's reign (check out his story in Genesis). Biblical prophecy said the king of Babylon would "shatter the obelisks of Heliopolis and burn the temple of the sun in fire" (Jeremiah 43:13). Today the city's ruins lie nearly 200 feet beneath the earth's surface.

City of the Sceptre

A luxurious city suitable for its royal citizens, **ancient Thebes** was the impressive capital of Upper Egypt. The Avenue of the Sphinxes connected two of the grandest temples there and was lined with 500 statues on either side.

Hieroglyph
Sceptre (Scepter)

FIT FOR KINGS

Forget Me Not

Kings wanted to stay in **pyramids**—not when they were living, of course, but after they died. So they built them. Royalty were buried in these distinctive tombs along with supplies and treasures for the "afterlife," like food, pets, thrones, and weapons.

DNA: With modern technology, scientists can take DNA samples from ancient bones and hair found in the pyramids to identify mummies and their relatives.

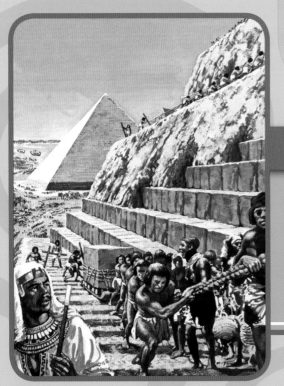

Technical Treasures

Pyramids are awesome structural accomplishments. Made of heavy stone, it took engineering whizzes and strong workers—thousands of strong workers—to construct them in a way that would last thousands of years.

A special infrared scan is used to find underground pyramids

AFP Photo/University of Alabama

Number's Up

More than 100 pyramids have been counted in Egypt. In 2011, archaeologists uncovered 17 more using NASA satellite imagery. They don't all look exactly the same, and some are in bad shape. For example, the pyramid at Meidum has lost four of its large, outer "steps" but still looks pretty good after hanging out in the sun and wind for more than 4,000 years!

Wikimedia Commons

REGAL TRIO

480 feet

755 feet

2.3 million blocks of stone

5.75 million tons

Crown Jewel

The oldest, grandest pyramid at Giza is called **The Great Pyramid**, built for King Khufu. It is not only the oldest of the Seven Wonders of the Ancient World, but it is the only one still standing. For nearly 4,000 years it was the tallest building in the world.

Sneak a Peek

Inside The Great Pyramid are only two small rooms. (A downward passageway goes to a third room below ground.) Above ground is the "queen's chamber," oddly named since it actually housed only a statue of the king. Inside the highest room, placed almost exactly in the middle of the pyramid, was the king's red granite sarcophagus.

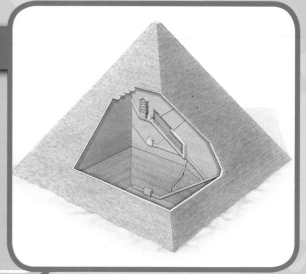

Maltings Partnership/DK Images/Getty Images

© WitR/Shutterstock

The Group at Giza

The most well-known pyramids are the three at **Giza**, named after the kings for whom they were built. This pyramid field includes smaller tombs thought to be for queens.

Shapely Shrines

Located across from the Israelite settlement at Goshen, the pyramids had already been standing for about 1,000 years when Abraham first came to Egypt. Biblical figures from Jacob to young Jesus probably checked out these same pyramids that countless visitors do today.

Duncan Walker/Getty Images

BURIED TREASURE

Royal Resting Place

Some pharaohs chose to be buried in the **Valley of the Kings**. Nearly 65 tombs have been uncovered here, some with many chambers. Experts believe more tombs have yet to be discovered.

Painted Places

Some of the most spectacular examples of Egyptian art cover the walls in the tombs of royalty. Tomb number 66 in the **Valley of the Queens** belongs to Nefertari, the beloved wife of popular Pharaoh Rameses II. The tomb walls of the seven rooms are carefully colored from corner to corner with pictures, prayers, and even a message from her husband.

© Dallet-Alba/Alamy

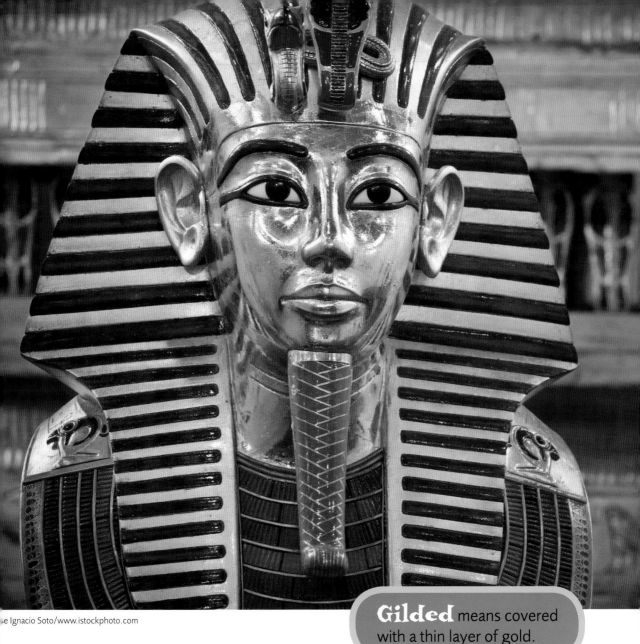

Gilded means covered with a thin layer of gold.

Dreamy Discovery

After searching for five years, archaeologist and Egyptologist Howard Carter discovered a sealed tomb that hadn't been disturbed for 3,000 years. Twenty-six feet underground, **King Tutankhamun's tomb** included four chambers packed with ancient treasures.

The burial room alone contained King Tut's mummy, covered by an elaborate "death mask," inside a solid gold coffin inside two increasingly larger gilded coffins, inside a red quartzite sarcophagus, inside four increasing larger gilded "shrines."

PRIZE FROM THE PAST

"Lion" Around

At the pyramids of Giza, an enormous statue called the **Great Sphinx** has kept watch for more than 4,000 years. A regal symbol of the day, it has the body of a crouching lion but the head of a king with a traditional Egyptian headdress.

The eyes of the Great Sphinx are taller than some grown men.

6 feet

Regal Creature

For years, desert sand buried the Great Sphinx, leaving only its awesome head above ground. Efforts were made throughout the centuries to uncover the stone statue, but it was not until the 1930s that it was completely revealed. At 240 feet long and 66 feet high, it is bigger than the Space Shuttle.

LC-USZ62-60317, LOC

© Pius Lee/Shutterstock

Battered and Bruised

Under the sand, the stone body of the Sphinx was protected from sun, wind, and humans. But the uncovered top of the statue has some scars. Its nose has been damaged and the cobra from the headdress is gone. The sphinx's ceremonial beard broke off and now has been reassembled and put on display in the British Museum.

KING SIZE

Huge Discoveries

Several ancient statues celebrating the powerful Pharaoh Rameses II still exist in Egypt. At Mit Rahina, a huge red granite statue of Rameses was found in six pieces. It was restored, strengthened with iron rods, and moved to a safer site. (Imagine moving a 36-foot statue that weighs as much as six school buses.)

Khaled Desouki/AFP/Getty Images

© Francois Gagnon/Shutterstock

Big Isn't Big Enough

At the temples in Abu Simbel, four huge statues show Rameses on his throne wearing the double crown of both Upper and Lower Egypt. Picture a six-story building. That's how tall each statue is.

Sleeping Giant

The broken feet of the **Colossus of Rameses** don't diminish this statue. The figure (nearly 33 feet) lies on its back giving lucky visitors an uncommon close-up view of Rameses' face.

Lost and Found

As late as 2004, the head, chest, and base of another statue were found in Akhmim. Do the math, adding up the measurements of each piece, and that intact statue would show the king as a very tall, 40-foot figure— and he is sitting!

PEEK INTO HISTORY

©1995 by Phoenix Data Systems

A Ruined View

The ruins at ancient **Thebes** include monuments, tombs, and entire temple complexes. The Great Hypostyle Hall has 122 engraved columns, 12 of them nearly 70 feet high each (taller than the columns at the Lincoln Memorial in Washington D.C.).

Dig It: Consider all the ruins that can't be seen. After all, shifting sands nearly buried the Great Sphinx, and the seas at Alexandria have covered Cleopatra's royal home. And in the Nile delta, archaeologists used radar imaging to find underground outlines of a city from 3,500 years ago when the Israelites were slaves. (Their story starts in Exodus 1.)

Memories of Memphis

© boonsom/www.123rf.com

In northern Egypt ruins of the busy, ancient city Memphis still stand. The Temples of Ptah, royal palaces, and huge statues show the grandeur of the former capital. The burial ground at **Saqqara** includes the oldest surviving pyramid of Djoser.

Rock Solid

In southern Egypt the rock temples of **Abu Simbel** draw thousands of visitors. They explore ancient inscriptions, paintings, and massive statues carved into the side of a mountain.

© takepicsforfun/Shutterstock

ART SMART

Tool Around

Early Egyptian civilization excelled at **metalwork**—mining metals, refining them, and forming them into heavy tools, fine jewelry, and delicate threads for cloth.

Paper Work

Ancient Egyptians used the abundant plant **papyrus** to make tough, thick paper. They separated parts of the plant, pounded and pressed it, and then dried it. While many people used scrolls, early Christian writers preferred papyrus sheets made into primitive books. Egyptians today still make papyrus for art and painting, not hieroglyphics.

Art Rules

Ancient Egyptian painting is very distinctive—flat and one-dimensional but by no means simple. Designs and wall paintings for nobility followed a rigid code of rules and meanings. Today, Egyptian art embraces variety.

PLAY ON

Music Makers

Four thousand years *before* Christ, Egyptians played harps, flutes called *neys*, and string instruments called *ouds*. Six hundred years *after* Christ, percussion and singing became popular. Today, Egyptian music shows the influences of ancient Egypt, Africa, and the Western world.

Z. Radovan/www.BibleLandPictures.com

AMR ABDALLAH DALSH/
Reuters /Landov

Good Sports

Soccer, known as **football** in Egypt, is all the rage both to play and to watch. Well-known Egyptian championship teams El Ahly and El Zamalek are popular worldwide. The Egyptian national teams won the African Cup of Nations a record seven times! In the early 1900s, Egypt excelled in weightlifting, boxing, and wrestling. Today, Egyptians compete in most sports including basketball, handball, squash, and tennis.

Wikimedia Commons

Belly Boogie

Raqs Sharqi (meaning "oriental dancing") might have originated in Egypt. Today the country is considered the international center for the art of the belly dance.

TIME FOR PRAYERS

Most Egyptians are **Muslim,** who worship in buildings called *mosques*. Each mosque has a *minaret* or tower. Five times a day, a call to prayer is issued from a mosque's minaret. Cairo, the capital of Egypt, is often called "The City of a Thousand Minarets."

Mark, author of the oldest gospel in the Bible, is traditionally considered the founder of the largest Christian church in Alexandria. The Coptic Church fulfills the prophecy of Isaiah 19:19—*"In that day there will be an altar to the LORD in the midst of the land of Egypt, and a pillar to the LORD at its border."*

Copt: A small number of Egyptians are **Coptic Christians**. The word *Copt* is an English word taken from the Arabic word *Gibt* or *Gypt*, which means "Egyptian."

PhotoDisc

TIME FOR PARTIES

Days of Dedication

Muslims celebrate two major holidays, *Eid-al-Fitr* and *Eid-al-Adha*. Coptic Christians recognize saints' days and Christmas, which they celebrate on January 7.

Romeo Gacad/AFP/Getty Images

Take a Break: The work week in Egypt is generally Sunday through Thursday. Friday and Saturday are the "weekend."

Khaled Desouki/AFP/Getty Images

Jump for July

Every year citizens celebrate the Egyptian Revolution of 1952. Revolution Day is similar to America's Independence Day (July 4), but Egypt's national holiday is July 23.

Take a Good Whiff

"Smelling of the breeze" is the literal translation of the *Sham-el-Nassim*, the festival which has been celebrated for thousands of years to mark the beginning of spring.

31

EAT, DRINK, AND MAKE SPICY

Cuisine Culture

For Egyptians, eating is almost always a social event.

A host will keep refilling a person's empty plate until it's left half full.

Although they don't usually drink with their meals, Egyptians enjoy thirst quenchers like *shai* (tea), tea with mint, mint steeped in hot water, and a hot or cold drink made from hibiscus flowers called *kirkadeh*.

© Madlen/Shutterstock

Tweet Treat

Hamam (pigeon) or *samaan* (quail) are often grilled and sprinkled with fresh lime, the same way they've been prepared since ancient times.

Koshari

Menu Favorites

Thick, strong Arabic coffee is a delight to those with iron stomachs.

Fava beans, known as *fuul,* make a hearty breakfast. Some keep it bland and some spice it up.

Spicy minced lamb *kofta* is ground meat made into patties or links and cooked.

Koshari features lentils on top of rice and macaroni, topped off with hot sauce and fried onions.

Um ali is a sweet mix of pastry, cream, coconut, raisins, and nuts. It makes a tasty dessert.

Um ali

Fishy Dish

In the spring Egyptians cure fish to make *fessikh*. Prepared correctly, it's pleasant. Prepared incorrectly, it can be poisonous.

OUT WITH THE OLD

Werner Forman/Universal Images Group/Getty Images

Pass It On

For much of its long history, Egypt was ruled by generations of royal families or *dynasties*. When a pharaoh died, his son took over, whose son eventually took over for him and so on. This is not the way Egypt is ruled today.

Over Ruled

For 3,000 years, Egypt was ruled by dynasties. Then Alexander the Great from Greece conquered Egypt 300 years before Christ was born. It stayed under foreign rule for more than 2,000 years. Then in 1952, a native Egyptian ruled once again.

Go Vote

Like America, Egypt is a republic where citizens vote for a president. The 28 *governorates* resemble states, which contain towns, cities, and local governing power.

© Iakov Filimonov/Shutters®

NEED TO LEAD

© 1995 by Phoenix Data Systems

You're Not Getting Any Younger

King Tutankhamun ruled for ten years before he died at age 19. Rameses II ruled for over 66 years and lived into his 90s.

Name Drop: Egypt played a vital role in many biblical events, yet only four pharaohs are named in the Bible.

Fine Line

Muhammad Naguib, one of the leaders of the Egyptian Revolution of 1952, became the first president on the day Egypt was declared a republic. Egyptian president number three, Anwar Sadat, governed for 11 years and won the Nobel Peace Prize. Egypt's fourth president, Hosni Mubarak, ruled for 30 years before he was forced to step down. In 2012, Mohamed Morsi was sworn into office.

Top (Naguib): Hulton Archive/Getty Images
Bottom (Morsi): Khaled Desouki/AFP/Getty Images

THERE'S NO PLACE LIKE HOME

In the Mix

Because Egypt lies between Europe, Africa, and Asia, it is a crossroad for many cultures. Minority groups living in Egypt include Nubians, Berbers, Bedouins, Arabs, Turks, Greeks, Bejas, and Doms. (Say that list ten times fast.)

Family Ties: A family-centered society, divorce was very uncommon in Egypt until recently.

© 1995 by Phoenix Data Systems

Welcome Mat

Travelers from all over the world come to experience the ancient wonders in Egypt. Native Egyptians are used to helping tourists find their way around.

© 1995 by Phoenix Data Systems

ش محمد مو...

ش الاسكندر الاكبر ◄

El Eskandar El Akbar St.

Say What?

Arabic is the official language of Egypt, but English and French are also widely spoken. German, Italian, and Spanish are common in certain places in Egypt as well.

Whipper-Snappers

As a whole, Egypt's population is young. In comparison, Germany, in Europe, just north of Egypt, has about four times the number of citizens who are 65 years old or older.

Need to Read

Males have a higher literacy rate than females, which means more boys than girls can read in Egypt.

FAMOUS VISITORS

French emperor **Napoleon Bonaparte** visited the pyramids at Giza in 1798 to survey the great structures.

English Prime Minister **Winston Churchill** attended conferences in Cairo in 1943.

Wikimedia Commons

Historical Time Period

Abram stays in Egypt

GENESIS 12:10

"Now there was a famine in the land, and Abram went down to Egypt to live there for awhile because the famine was severe."

Joseph rises to power and Jacob's family moves to Egypt

GENESIS 47:11

"So Joseph settled his father and his brothers in Egypt and gave them property in the best part of the land, the district of Rameses, as Pharaoh directed."

Moses is born ar leads the Israelit out of Egypt

© Providence Collection/GoodSalt

Old Kingdom
51 years

Middle Kingdom
243 years

New Kingdo
323 years

American **Franklin D Roosevelt** was the first US president to visit Egypt, in 1943. Sixty-six years later the 44th US president, **Barack Obama**, met with Egyptian president Hosni Mubarak.

Russian president **Vladimir Putin** became the first Russian leader in 40 years to make an official state visit to Egypt, in 2005.

Australian singer **Kylie Minogue**, French performer **Jean Michael Jarre**, American rock band **Grateful Dead**, and the Aida opera have all performed at the Giza pyramids.

(C)2010 Ron Sachs from Consolidated News Photos

© Lars Justinen/GoodSalt

Hebrew prophet Jeremiah dies in Egypt

Young Jesus enters Egypt with his family

MATTHEW 2:13
"When they had gone, an angel of the Lord appeared to Joseph in a dream. 'Get up,' he said, 'take the child and his mother and escape to Egypt. Stay there until I tell you, for Herod is going to search for the child to kill him.'"

Duncan Walker/Getty Images

Late Period
302 years

Roman Rule

CRACK THE CODE

Write Right

The word **hieroglyph** (rhymes with *high go cliff*) comes from a Greek word that means "sacred carving." It refers to a symbol or picture in the formal writing system of **hieroglyphics**.

© Kudryasha/Shutterstock

© The Power of Forever Photography/www.istockphoto.com

A Lot to Learn

When experts figured out what the hieroglyphic pictures were and what the symbols meant using the Rosetta Stone, they learned (and are still learning) about people and events that would have been long forgotten. Now they can confirm events in the Bible, explore beliefs and battles, and understand decisions and declarations.

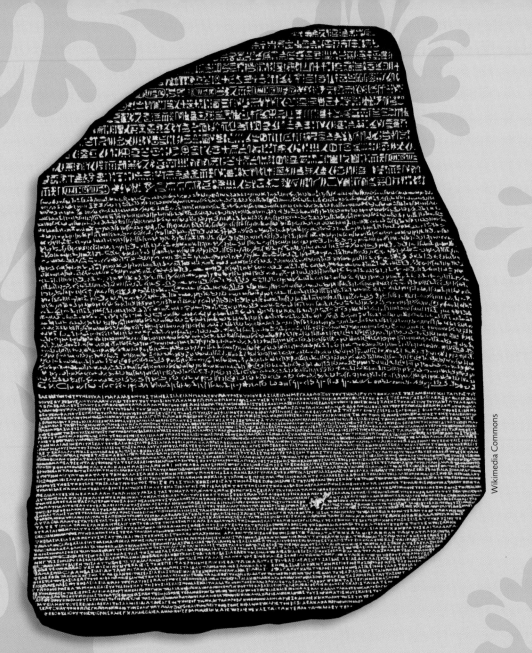

Set in Stone

For centuries, experts couldn't figure out the meanings of hieroglyphics. Then 200 years ago, a key to the code was discovered! A big black tablet was found in the northern city of Memphis. It included the same message in three languages. Since historians knew two of the languages, they could compare it to the ancient writing they didn't know. They basically had a Greek translation of ancient hieroglyphics. This rare find, the **Rosetta Stone**, is as tall as a five-year-old child but weighs 1,700 pounds.

BEASTS OF THE FIELD

Long Gone

A number of animals that are featured in ancient Egyptian art no longer exist in Egypt, including hippos, giraffes, and ostriches. Even crocodiles are now found only south of the Aswân High Dam.

Desert Dwellers

The largest wild animal in Egypt is a bearded sheep or *aoudad* (pronounced "Ow, Dad!"). The Nubian ibex and Dorcas gazelle share the desert with small foxlike animals called *fennecs* and two kinds of *jerboa* (a mouse-like rodent with long hind legs for jumping).

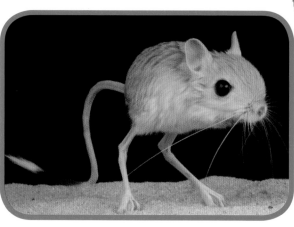

© reptiles4all/Shutterstock

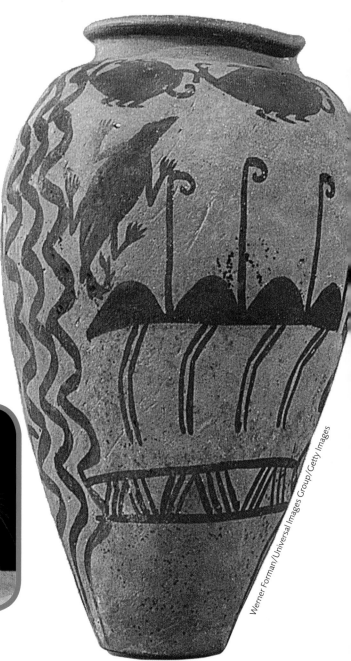

Werner Forman/Universal Images Group/Getty Images

42

© Attila Jandi/Shutterstock

Let Me Introduce You

The furry hyrax is found in the mountains of the Sinai Peninsula. English translators had never heard of this animal, so in early translations of the Bible, the words "rabbit" and "hare" were mistakenly used.

I Want My Mummy

At first glance the Caffre cat looks like a pet curled up on the couch. But this is no house cat. The Egyptian wildcat cleared out mice and snakes and became the symbol of grace and poise. In 1888, a tomb containing cats carefully wrapped in linen was discovered, proving that Egyptians often prized their cats.

Mary Evans Picture Library

COLD-BLOODED CREATURES

Clammy Companions

Nearly 50 species of lizards live in Egypt. Most are geckos which can be measured in inches. On the other hand, Egypt's largest lizard, the Nile monitor, can grow longer than your dad is tall.

© BruceBlock/www.istockphoto.com

Don't Say Goodbye

Once common along the Nile, the crocodile is now found only in Lake Nasser, along with the large monitor and the soft-shelled turtle. Five species of sea turtles found in Egyptian waters are endangered.

© Ahmed Abdalla/Grant Heilman Photography

Shy and Scaly

Snakes help keep mice, rats, and other pests from taking over an area. About half of the 36 snake species in Egypt are poisonous.

Freaky Features

One look at the sharp points behind its eyes, and it's no wonder where the poisonous Horned Viper got its name. When the cobra gets annoyed, it flattens its neck region into a "cape" and adopts a classic upright cobra pose. The spitting cobra can shoot blinding venom six feet. The sand viper slithers sideways to go forward.

© Eric Isselee/Shutterstock

CREEPY-CRAWLY CROWD

Big Buggy Deal

To the ancient Egyptian, a bug's behavior had significance and religious symbolism. Important insects are found in tomb drawings and on jewelry, seals, and amulets (which are like lucky charms).

Jumping Jehosophat

Grasshoppers, or locusts, which travel in swarms, represented a king's enemies as in "soldiers came into the city like locusts." Pharaoh Rameses II wrote a similar description for his Hittite enemies.

© Paul Fleet/Shutterstock

© Oktay Ortakcioglu/
www.istockphoto.com

Wikimedia Commons

Beetles Are the Bomb

Scarabs take dung, or animal poop, and roll it into perfectly round balls. To the ancient Egyptians, this symbolized a god rolling the sun across the sky. At the Temple of Karnak, a colossal dung beetle carved from red granite rests on top of a high, carved pedestal.

Buzz on Over

Large golden figures of flies were awards for toughness in battle just like we award trophies today. The museum in Cairo owns three that were found in a queen's tomb, apparently gifts from her sons who earned the prized flies.

Werner Forman Archive/The Bridgeman Art Library

Fancy Flyers

Butterflies were not a religious symbol as much as a symbol of beauty. Like honeybees, they inspired jewelry and colorful tomb paintings.

© Masterfile

Hieroglyph

Can you guess these insects from their hieroglyph symbol?

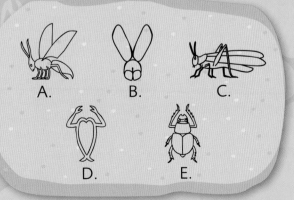

A.

B.

C.

D.

E.

ANSWERS: A.bee; B.fly; C.locust; D.water scorpion; E.dung beetle

GLOSSARY

Ancient: Belonging to the very distant past and no longer in existence

Archaeologist: An expert who studies ancient people and their culture

Artifacts: An object made by a human being, typically of cultural or historic interest

Colossal: Extremely large

Colossus: A statue that is much bigger than life size

Delta: A triangular area of deposits at the mouth of a river

Famine: Extreme shortage of food in a region

Native: Connected with the country or region of a person's birth. For example, a native of Egypt is born in Egypt.

Obelisk: A stone pillar (typically a square pillar with a pyramidal top) set up as a monument or landmark

© Holger Mette/www. istockphoto.com

Peninsula: A piece of land projecting out into a body of water

Pharaoh: A ruler in ancient Egypt

Sarcophagus: A stone coffin, typically displayed above ground

Sceptre: A fancy staff carried by rulers on ceremonial occasions as a symbol of power

© Markov/Dreamstime

Shrine: A container for honored objects

Steps (like on a pyramid): Flat platforms built from the ground, from larger to smaller, to achieve a completed shape similar to a geometric pyramid

© Arthur R./Shutterstock